150 Life Lessons for Leavers

&

Life-Long Learners

Making the most of your final year at school
… and the rest of your life

James B. DEPIAZZI

Copyright © James Depiazzi, 2020
Published: January 2020 by
The Book Reality Experience

ISBN: 978-0-6487188-2-6
Paperback Edition

All rights reserved.

The right of James Depiazzi to be identified as the author of this Work has been asserted by him in accordance with sections 77 and 78 of the Copyright, Designs and Patents Act 1988.

The information contained in this book is of a general nature and should not be regarded as legal advice or relied on for assistance in any particular circumstance or emergency situation. It is not intended as and should not be relied upon for legal or medical advice. The publisher and author are not responsible for any specific needs that may require professional supervision. If you have any doubts about the advice contained in this book, you should contact a qualified appropriate professional.

The Publisher and author jointly or singularly, accept no responsibility or liability for any damage, loss or expense incurred as a result of the reliance on information contained in this guide.

Any third party views or recommendations included in this guide do not reflect the views of the Publisher or indicate its commitment to a particular course of action.

No part of this publication may be reproduced, stored in a retrieval system, copied in any form or by any means, electronic, mechanical, photocopying, recording or otherwise transmitted without written permission from the publisher. You must not circulate this book in any format.

Cover design: Web and Print Hub | www.webandprinthub.com.au

To all of the Leavers
who have been a part of my classes
and a part of my life
for more than thirty years

and for my son Dominic
who was a Leaver
in 2016

This book is a collection of life lessons, questions and quotes
to accompany you on the journey through your last year at school
and throughout the years ahead.

Because there is more to life than what they teach you at school.
Where do you learn all of those little life lessons
that are so important for happiness and success?

Drawn from over thirty-five years of teaching experience,
parenting and numerous self-help and life-coaching books and courses,
these lessons cover everything from goal setting and time management,
to networking and housework, financial literacy and motivation.

Learning these lessons is a lifelong process.
They don't stop when you finish school.

NB *Your life is different to everyone else's, so your book should be different too. Take time to colour in and comment on your book.*

Answer the questions, doodle, highlight your favourite bits, and make notes. There's space at the back to add your own lessons.

Introduction

I have been a teacher for over thirty-five years now, but that has never stopped me from learning. In fact, I was a learner long before I began teaching and the more I teach, the more lessons I need to learn.

This book contains a few of those life lessons that I wanted to pass on to my children, students and friends in the hope that they can learn from them.

My original idea was that it would be a kind of journal to accompany leaving students through their final year of school. There is one lesson for each school day of three, ten-week terms. I hoped that students would write in it and keep it afterwards as a memento and a reminder of the lessons that they had learned along the way.

I also envisioned teachers using this book as a guide for journal writing or reflection with their classes.

As the concept developed, I realised that many of the ideas had a wider application beyond the classroom. I added '& Life-Long Learners' to the title – nothing like a little more alliteration!

This book is for everybody who still has something to learn.

That's all of us.

James D

PS Do not think that I have mastered all of these life lessons yet. I haven't. Some of them have helped to shape my life in significant ways. Many are lessons that I am still learning. After all, they are 'life' lessons and I am not dead yet.

Do not be too hard on yourself. Do what works for you now and save some for later on. Be a life-long learner (#150).

1 - Be prepared to start

Draw up a checklist of what you need to have or do to get started, then get it ready. Chefs call this mise-en-place or simply the 'Meez'. It is a way of avoiding any rude surprises or missing ingredients halfway through a cooking project.

Make sure that you have all of the correct books and equipment that you need. Label your things.

Have your uniform/clothes ready. Prepare your lunch.

Tidy your desk, set up a filing system, have your timetable clearly displayed, set your alarm. Get a good sleep.

A job well started is half finished. Start the year on a positive note!

How prepared do I feel?

The journey of a thousand miles
begins with a single step.
Lao Tzu

2 - Set Goals

Where are you going to? What do you want to achieve?

Having goals written down is proven to lead to better life outcomes. Several well-known studies show this. Something about writing your goals down makes them more real, more engaging and more tangible. Take time to write down some of the things that you want to do and be. Be realistic, but set yourself some challenges too. Be specific so that you can tell when you have achieved your goals.

Prepare some long, medium and short term goals. Get into the habit of setting goals regularly e.g. each day, week, month and term. This book will help by reminding you of this.

What did I enjoy doing today?

Having a goal changes your perspective,
your approach, your way of looking at things.
It adds purpose to what would otherwise be empty minutes.

3 - Set up a Weekly Study Guide

Plan weekly with time allocated for all of the tasks that you have to complete for each of the roles in your life e.g. as a student, a son or daughter, friend, worker, sportsperson, etc. Include all of your commitments to yourself and others.

Doing this each week gives you something to look forward to and aim for; it lets you know when you can fit it in and when you have time to do other things.

Make sure that you keep a balance between school, work, health, relationships and any other activity that is important to you.

What do I have planned to do today?

Not having a plan is like planning to fail.
Imagine trying to build a house without a floorplan.
Surely our lives are important enough to plan for?

4 - Use ten minutes wisely

We often think that we need big chunks of time to get a job done, and so never start. The reality is that we should break big jobs down into smaller parts for which we CAN find time. It is good to make a list of things that you can do during those short periods that we have each day: at the end of a class, waiting for transport, between appointments, before you go to bed, while talking on the phone.

Think in terms of two minute jobs (making a note in your diary, looking up the meaning of a word, giving a hug), five minute jobs (a quick Thank You note or phone call, making a snack, checking emails) and ten minute jobs (a brisk walk, bringing in the washing, putting the dishes away, tidying a shelf in your room, filing paperwork).

All of those little times add up to make a substantial difference to your productivity day after day.

What could I do in ten minutes today?

Life is made up of little blocks of time all joined together.
Every ten minutes is an important part of your life.
Don't waste your time!

5 - Review the week

What went well? Can you do this again?
What would you change or do differently?
When did you feel happiest? Saddest? Most fulfilled?
What matters most to you?

Make time to do a review like this each week, month and term, if not every day!

What did I learn about myself this week?

The unexamined life is not worth living.
Socrates

6 - Set up a Tickler File

This is a great little strategy for managing paperwork. Also called The 43 Folders, this simple filing system keeps you organised and makes sure that you don't miss deadlines, payments or anniversaries. No more nasty surprises. No more lost assessments or paperwork.

Organise thirty-one folders numbered 1-31 for each day of the month and twelve other folders; one labelled for each month of the year from January to December. The months are ordered from the current month onwards and the dates from today to the end of the month. Each day the front folder is checked and then moved back to the next month. Paperwork is filed according to the date (within the next month) or month (within the next year) that it needs to be acted on. If you want, you can add an extra folder for longer-term considerations, but planning a year ahead is more than most people need or do.

How do I manage paperwork?

Paper wrangling is still an essential skill
even in our so-called 'paperless' society.
Having a good system saves time and worry.

7 - What is the Next Action?

Do it now! Don't procrastinate! Getting started is the hardest part, but just doing something is the first step – like writing the first word on the first page of a new book. As Lao-tzu said, the journey of a thousand miles begins with a single step ... and then another and another ...

Big tasks need to be broken down or 'chunked' into manageable, 'doable' pieces e.g. locating a single resource, making a phone call, defining a term, viewing a documentary, conducting an interview, etc.

Most tasks are easier in the doing than the contemplating. What is the next ACTION step for you?

What is the next action step for me now?

Happiness rarely comes to those who just wait.
We need to take action and be proactive
to achieve anything worthwhile.

8 - Healthy Body, Healthy Mind

We are not disembodied creatures. Our brain is a part of this whole complex organism that makes us who we are. What we eat, how we sit, how much sleep and exercise we get impact on our moods and our thinking. To be at our best mentally, we need to look after our body. If you don't know how to do this, there are plenty of resources available about caring for yourself and being healthy. It is hard enough to motivate yourself to work and study without sabotaging your efforts by not caring for yourself properly.

How can I take better care of my body today?

Our body is the vehicle
that we use to travel through the journey of life.
Like any vehicle, it needs regular care and maintenance.

9 - Work WITH your body clock

I grew up on a dairy farm, so early mornings work well for me. I am most alert and efficient in the early hours of the day. That is when I do most of my writing. My friend Mark did his best work between 10 pm and 1 am

What is your best time? When do you feel most focused and ready to learn? It makes sense to note when you are at your sharpest mentally and then to make use of that time to do your best work.

When do I do my best work?

For everything there is a season,
a time for every activity under heaven.
Ecclesiastes 3:1

10 - Keep the end in mind

After just two weeks, it is good to look back and review how you are going. To do this, keep the end in mind. Where are you wanting to get to? How have your activities so far helped in achieving this goal? Are there distractions or problems that you need to sort out now before you get too far behind? Do you need to rethink your goals or just approach them differently? It is early days, but a job well started is half done. If you haven't started well, it is time to reset and start again today!

How am I honestly travelling so far?

Regular, honest reviews keep us on track.
Don't be afraid to make changes by choice
rather than waiting until you are made to change.

11 - Begin each day with achievement

Our attitude often determines the quality of our experience. If you can, begin your day by doing something positive then you set the tone for the day. It may be exercise, study, reading or meditation, but getting something meaningful or enjoyable done before breakfast helps to kick-start your day. You may want to do the same thing or set a different activity for each day. Just do something that gives you a feeling of achievement and momentum as you start out.

What will I do to kick-start my day tomorrow?

*Good habits and decisions
shape our minds and bodies
for the day ahead.*

12 - Choose your friends wisely

The research is clear: we become like the people we associate with. Whether it is your income level, your health, habits, language or attitudes, the people around you have more influence than you think. If you want to succeed and achieve good results, choose friends who also have those goals.

From the book of Proverbs in the Bible to personal and professional development best sellers, the message is clear: listen to your parents when they caution you to be careful of the company you keep. Take their advice. Choose your friends wisely.

In what ways do my friends influence me ... honestly?

Make no friendship with a man given to anger,
nor go with a wrathful man,
lest you learn his ways
and entangle yourself in a snare.
Proverbs 22: 24-25

13 - Discover the power of the Pareto Principle

Also known as the 80/20 rule, this principle describes how we tend to spend our time and energy. In simple terms, we spend 20% of our time doing 80% of our work. This is most obvious when a deadline is approaching, and we suddenly improve our productivity. The other 80% of our time is spent doing the other 20% of our work or thinking about it! Proponents of this idea suggest that we can improve our productivity considerably if we create a 'deadline mentality' – giving ourselves time limits and targets to achieve so that we are more focused and efficient rather than casually approaching tasks with no real sense of urgency or no end date in mind.

What motivates me to work more efficiently?

*We all want to discover the most efficient way
to work or make money.
Could we also aim to live more efficiently?*

14 - Paper wrangling

Keeping on top of the paper war is crucial.
Here are a few tried principles you may like to adopt:
Handle each document or piece of paper once.
Put your name and date on every handout you receive.
Have a place for everything (see The Tickler File – Life Lesson #6).

How can I improve my paper wrangling?

It is not because things are difficult that we do not dare,
it is because we do not dare that they are difficult.
Seneca

15 - Power naps rule!

My grandfather had a nap after lunch nearly every day and many famous people like Albert Einstein, Salvador Dali, Winston Churchill and Thomas Edison were renowned for taking naps. It is a habit I have also employed with great success.

Naps can vary in length from mere minutes to over an hour, and each has its own benefits. It seems that shorter naps of 10-20 minutes are most effective and help to avoid that groggy feeling that you get after falling asleep for too long. You can use an alarm to avoid over-doing it! Even a six minute nap can help.

Benefits from naps include enhanced memory, increased alertness, improved motor learning, better decision making and more creative problem solving.

But a word of warning: don't try taking a nap during classes!

Am I getting enough sleep?

*Sleep is still the best medicine
and it is free!*

16 - Keep a sense of proportion

How much will this matter in five years' time? We all make mistakes and do embarrassing things, but in the long run they rarely matter. Most people can't remember what they did last week. This whole year and the exams and any other issues you have right now are just a small part of a much bigger picture: your life! One day you will look back on all of this and wonder what all of the fuss was about ... if you even remember it that is!

What did I do last week that was truly memorable?

You will be surprised at how much you forget,
but you may not even remember this!

17 - 'What will you do when you finish school?'

Be prepared for this question because you are going to get sick of hearing it from well-meaning adults, over and over again this year.

Have an answer ready – even if you don't know exactly what you want to do. At least sound like you have given it some thought. 'I don't know' usually leads to further interrogation and suggestions. Better to have a stock standard answer about a gap year, possible university courses, a job you would like or travel plans.

It is also useful to pursue answers to this question for yourself – having something to aim for is a great motivator and gives you a sense of purpose and direction.

What WILL I do when I finish school?

It is OK if you don't know what you want to do
as long as you are still actively looking for the answer.
'I don't know' is not a good long-term proposition.

18 - Read for Pleasure

All work and no play makes Jack a dull boy (or leaves Jill feeling jaded). Don't forget to read for pleasure, or to make time for whatever other small pleasures add to the richness and enjoyment of life for you … a bike ride, computer games, cooking, singing or horse-riding. Your academic results this year are important, but pursuing them shouldn't be all consuming. Most authorities agree that taking time out to do what you love or just to relax will actually improve your performance, not detract from it!

Which book will I start reading this week?

People with ideas, knowledge and experience write books
so that you can learn from them
without all of the hassles along the way.

19 - Do it in two!

If you have a small job to do that will take less than two minutes to do, do it NOW!

What can I do in two minutes?

A two minute hug can make your day ... or someone else's.

20 - Analyse the first few weeks

How are you doing so far? What is going well? What do you need to improve? What is missing? What do you need help with? Who can you ask for help? What changes do you want to make? Do you feel that you are making progress in the right direction? What are you proud of? What do you need to stop doing?

What is the main thing that I have learned so far?

*Human beings have been blessed
with the ability to think, grow, imagine, create and change.
Use your human gifts today!*

21 - Be inspired!

When I was a student I had a copy of an inspirational verse on my bedroom wall. Each day I would read it through. In many ways it was my life guide.

Perhaps you could sign up to a daily motivational quote or app. Start each day with a great idea or a new way of thinking. One lived sentence can change your life – choose one that works for you.

What sentence or saying inspires me the most?

*One idea lived well
can be the foundation for a worthwhile life.*

22 - Do a time audit

Each week contains 168 hours.
Each person has the same amount of time each week
How do YOU use your time?
Do an audit of your time use over the next week. Simply write down everything that you do and how long it takes.
What does this say about what you value?

How do I feel about how I use my time?

*All of the great and famous people who have ever lived
have had the same number of hours per day as the rest of us.
Time is more about priority and passion than minutes and hours.*

23 - Home Work

Traditional homework is a controversial topic in education circles and philosophies vary markedly. Developing self-discipline, reviewing previous work and learning how to study efficiently are obviously of value, especially if you intend pursuing tertiary studies; but this should not be the end of the discussion.

Another approach is to expand the concept of home work to include work that is done at or around the home: contributing to your family, developing useful life skills, keeping fit, caring for pets or the young or elderly, reading for pleasure, playing music and sport, learning a language or an instrument, earning some money or volunteering.

What work should I do at home tonight?

*Doing chores and helping out at home
are not a form of punishment or slavery.
They are ways to develop useful skills
and to contribute to our families and communities.*

24 - Keep an empty head (and an open mind).

Write down EVERYTHING that needs to be done, not just homework and deadlines. Write down ideas and plans, goals and dreams. Doing this leaves you with a clear head and means that you have space to think and be creative without the stress and worry that comes from trying to remember everything.

If you are worried about something, write that down too. By describing and defining the problem clearly on paper, you may find that it looks far more manageable. You might sleep better too if you get your worries out of your head.

What have I been worrying about lately?

Words on paper
make fuzzy thinking clearer
and big problems smaller.

25 - Do what works

Some people say that there are only two ways to do anything: the right way and the wrong way. This is rarely true. There is often a third way and then there are variations on all of these. Find your own ways to do things. Find what works for you. If you are a left-hander you have often done this already, but others can do this too. Try a different angle, a new technique, an alternative grip or a change in the order or sequence of events or procedures. Adapt an activity or workspace to suit your interests and body type. Look at life differently and do what works for you.

What can I do differently that works for me?

*If it is legal and moral and ethical
AND it works for you,
do it that way.*

26 - Just do ONE thing well

This idea keeps coming up in self-help books: What is the ONE thing that if you did it properly and did it regularly would make a positive difference to your school, work or home life? Eating well? Exercising? Remembering names? Avoiding procrastination?

Research suggests that multi-tasking is a myth – it is having a focus that makes us more productive and effective.

Choose one thing each day, week, month, term or year ... then just do it!

What is ONE thing that I could do today to make a positive difference in my life?

*There are lots of things that are important to do,
but I can't do them all.
Choosing something to focus on
ensures that at least one important thing gets done.*

27 - Think ahead

When the European Space Agency's Rosetta spacecraft's Philae lander touched down on the comet 67P/Churyumov-Gerasimenko on 12th August 2014, it was an awesome scientific achievement, but it didn't just happen. It took sixteen years from planning and production, including six years of travelling about 6.4 billion kilometres through space, to arrive at the moment that made headlines around the world. Where do you want to be in sixteen years? What do you need to do now to start heading in that direction? Do it.

What step will I take towards my future today?

*Living in the present
does not mean not planning ahead.
Every house is built on what was once an empty block of land.*

28 - First World Problems

This popular term began as a way of describing things that were annoying or inconvenient (like a broken fingernail or a flat tyre), but that when compared to third world problems, shrunk into insignificance. They were hardly life threatening or even memorable. It was another way of saying 'get a grip' or 'build a bridge'! Don't let minor setbacks get out of perspective. The sun will still rise tomorrow.

What can I learn from the events of this day?

*Problems can easily get out of perspective,
but they usually hold more opportunities
than pain.*

29 - Be Different

No one else is just like you, so you should be different from everybody else. In what ways are you different? What could people say about you that wouldn't be true of any other human being?

Over time I have developed several little 'markers' that, put together, help people to recognise and remember me as an individual. I sign my name with a smiley face (even on legal documents). I stick postage stamps on at an angle. I write poetry and wear an old bush hat when I read it. I enjoy power naps. When I was younger my drink of preference was milk. I don't drink coffee or a well-known brand of cola, but I do have a liking for polar fleece vests, and I have an extensive tie collection. My bike is distinctive. I cut up my toast differently. I have published a book.

How do you differentiate yourself from the crowd?

What makes me different?

No one else can be you.
You owe it to yourself to be your best self.

30 - Be Prepared

In a few short months you will be finishing school. Are you ready for the next stage of your life?

In particular, do you have the basic home/life skills that you may need? Can you wash (and iron) your own clothes? Change a car tyre, tap washer or light globe? Access and manage money? Prepare meals? Use a bus/train timetable? Care for a pet?

You might like to draw up a list of skills to work on between now and graduation/leavers.

What life skill can I work on this week?

*Freedom is one of our greatest desires.
Being dependent on others for simple daily needs
takes away our most basic freedom and independence.*

31 - Make Small Changes

Making big changes is difficult. Most of us struggle to develop new habits or to improve our performance significantly.

The secret is to start small.

If you can improve by one third of one per cent (0.33%) per day you would improve by over 120% per year!

Great things come from small beginnings. Doing a little bit more study or exercise or reading each day is not too difficult … and the more we do the easier it gets.

What small change can I commit to today?

Each little step, choice or decision
moves us closer to our goal,
makes us a better person
and makes the next step easier.

32 - Keep perspective

It is easy to get caught up in the tragedy or drama of news stories about natural disasters, political upheavals or economic chaos.

As the headlines and TV news switch into frenzy mode, it is important to maintain perspective. It helps to imagine that you are out camping without access to media or communication devices. How would this event really impact on your life?

I'm not advocating selfishness or lack of interest in current affairs, but in the end, does it really matter to your life now? Why fret over things that you cannot change or control and that probably won't impact you directly anyway?

What was I worrying about five years ago?

So much of what concerns us is not our concern.
What really matters in the end
is a lot less than we think.

33 - Avoid noise

At its most basic level, excessive noise can damage your hearing. This can come from huge concert speakers in the mosh pit or from earbuds pumping out your favourite tunes so loud that others around you can hear them too. Once the damage is done, it cannot be reversed. Look after your hearing.

At a more subtle level, noise disturbs us. We all have noises that irritate, annoy or enrage us. I hate the sound of vacuum cleaners and washing machines. But even less intrusive background noise keeps us on edge, in a heightened state of alert. This can increase anxiety and tension without us even being aware of it. Make some space for quiet in your life. Turn off music and appliances. Spend time in nature. Give yourself the gift of peace and quiet.

What can I hear at this moment?

*When you arise in the morning,
think of what a precious privilege it is to be alive –
to breathe, to think, to enjoy, to love.*
Marcus Aurelius

34 - Enjoy the gift of each day!

It doesn't matter which day of the week it is; each day is a gift. For some people this is the first day of their lives. For others it is the last. Each day is precious. Don't waste a single one. This day has been given to you as a gift. You can do what you like with it but be grateful for the opportunities it brings and don't let it end with regret for what you should have done.

Tomorrow is too late to live today!

What am I going to do with this day?

*Today
is the only day that matters.
This is the only day of my life.*

35 - Act on your values

Make a list of your values. What is important to you?

Next to each item, write down what you actually do to show that you value that thing, for example, if you value your health you might exercise several times a week. If you care about poverty you may volunteer or give money to charity. If you love music, you may spend time learning to play a musical instrument or you might save money to pay for lessons.

How we spend our time, money and energy shows what we really value. Does your life reflect your values? How do you feel about this?

Living by our values makes us more authentic, develops strength of character and leads to a greater sense of satisfaction with life.

What values have been reflected in my life this week?

Nothing is as valuable as integrity.
Living authentically
has a power of its own.

36 - Maintain your standards

You need to get a licence to drive on the roads. There is a base level of skills and knowledge necessary to share the roads safely with others.

You should also maintain certain standards in your day-to-day life, which you share with those around you.

It may be as simple as brushing your teeth, or your hair, each morning. Keeping your shirt tucked in or putting dirty clothes into the laundry. Saying please and thank you. Leaving the bathroom tidy for the next person. Not swearing. Not spreading gossip. Being on time. Not skipping breakfast. Getting assessments in on time. Acknowledging family birthdays. Paying for fuel that you have used.

Your dignity and self-respect as a person depend on having standards that you will not compromise.

What are my basic standards?

There are some things that I do
because I believe that is what should be done.
I don't need to be told to do them.
They are a part of who I am and how I operate.

37 - Do what you love

You may have heard the saying, 'Do what you love, and you will never work a day of your life'. Hopefully you can find a way to make money from it too!

So what do you love? What are you passionate about? What attracts and interests and inspires you? What would you love to do even if you didn't get paid?

You are more likely to succeed if you love what you do. You will find the energy and resources and persistence that are needed for achievement.

If you don't know what you love to do, keep trying new things until you find something that fascinates and stimulates your mind and your heart.

What do I most love to do?

*Time hardly seems to pass
when we are engaged in doing what we love,
and there is no better feeling
than that timeless pursuit.*

38 - Planning for your fortieth (or eightieth)

You may be looking forward to turning 18 or 21 but getting to 40 (or 80) years old seems like a distant dream. Just the same, imagine it is your fortieth birthday tomorrow and some of your closest friends and family members are going to get up to speak about you and your life.

What will they say?

What would you like them to say?

Each passing day brings you closer to that celebration and all of the actions and relationships in your life shape those future speeches. You can choose what they will say by what you do and say each day.

What would I like people to say about me?

We build our life each day.
Those days add up to something.
What are your days adding up to?

39 - Gift experiences

Being a cash-poor student, expensive gifts are often unaffordable, but you can give non-material gifts like sharing time or skills with another person. Teach them about technology or music, play cards or a board game, give them a shoulder massage, do gardening or cooking for them or watch a favourite movie together.

Something as simple as a genuine hug or a leisurely stroll along the beach at sunset makes a lasting gift and a cherished memory.

What experience could I gift to someone?

*Giving the gift of an experience
builds relationships
and honours life
more than things will.*

40 - No Excuses

Excuses are not very helpful. They are a way of avoiding responsibility for our own lives and actions. Growing up means accepting responsibility. If you find yourself repeatedly making excuses for being late, losing things, not handing work in on time or forgetting promises or appointments, then it is time to take a good hard look at yourself.

What do you need to change about your attitude, record keeping, time management, or decision making processes? It is up to you. Don't blame others for things that you can control and change.

What excuses do I need to own up to?

*Owning up
instead of making excuses
is a sure sign
of growing up.*

41 - Set it up

If you have a job that you need to start, but it is too late to do it before the end of the day or you have to go out somewhere else first, at least set it up so that you can start it first thing in the morning or when you get back. Have all of the books or clothes or tools that you need out and ready so that you can make the most of your time. Getting started is usually the hardest part of any task, so make it easier for yourself by having everything set up and ready to go.

What should I set up for before going to bed tonight?

*Setting up saves time,
sets the tone
and prepares our mind for the next task.*

42 - Nagging is caring

You are probably getting sick of being asked if you have done your homework or if you have study to do. Parents are often guilty of what teenagers call 'nagging'. Why do they do that?

It may be annoying and hard to hear, but it is really another way of caring. It is their way of letting you know that they care about you and want what is best for you. Ask yourself, 'do they have a reason to be concerned?' If not, you might reassure them that you are actually doing enough work and achieving good results so they can ease back on the questions. On the other hand, they may have a point and you may need to lift your game and get more focused on your work. Perhaps you could thank them for caring enough to keep you on task.

Who cares enough to nag me?

*That which annoys us the most
often has the most to teach us.*

43 - Clear your desk

There is a lot of evidence to suggest that a clean desk leads to clearer thinking. De-cluttering our surroundings is a healthy way to clear our minds as well. Get rid of things that you don't need or use. Remove distractions. Reduce the time wasting that comes from not being able to find what you need. A few minutes each day maintaining a tidy workspace will pay dividends in increased focus and efficiency.

What can I clear from my desk today?

*Space
is the new frontier
that can be explored
when you clear away the clutter
in your life.*

44 - Let it go

Before it became a hit song from the movie Frozen, this was a sensible philosophy of life.

So often we hold on to things from the past: insults, hurts, mistakes and embarrassing moments. We hold on to them and replay them in our minds and our imaginations.

It is time to let them go and move on. We cannot change the past, but letting go of those things can make space for change and improve the future for us.

What past burden do I need to let go of so that I can move forward?

It makes sense to lighten your load
in as many ways as possible.
Let go of what is holding you back
emotionally, financially, physically and socially.

45 - Record your ideas

Ideas are funny things. They come and go. If you want to remember your best ideas, write them down or record them digitally. Carry a pen and paper or some kind of device to capture your insights and ideas as soon as they occur. Plan your day. Solve problems. List responses. Write songs or poetry. Don't risk losing your brain's best work.

When do I get my best ideas?

*The best intentions
are not as good
as the smallest actions.*

46 - Take another path

Wherever you go and whatever you do, there is usually an alternative way of getting there or doing it. Going to school, going shopping, travelling to holidays or another town? Try another way. Take a scenic drive. Explore side roads. Use an alternative means of transport. Break the journey with a stopover.

Humans tend to be creatures of habit. It is good to challenge ourselves; to open our minds to new ways of thinking, to see situations and problems differently.

Life is often painted as black and white with limited choices, but it is really more complex and interesting than this. Cultivating a richer appreciation of life begins with thinking, seeing and doing things differently.

What can I do differently today?

*Breaking habits
is a habit worth cultivating.*

47 - Smile for the camera

Very few people seem to like photos of themselves. As a result they don't like people taking photos of them and they don't 'smile for the camera'. This becomes a self-fulfilling prophecy.

My theory is that the more photos you have taken, the higher the chance of getting a good one! Smile for the camera and enjoy the experience. In years to come you will be happy to look back through old school magazines and social media posts to see your happy, smiling face surrounded by good friends.

What impression would people get from photos of me?

A smile makes up
for a lack of make-up,
but no amount of make-up
can make up for the lack of a smile.

48 - Be money smart

Schools don't usually teach us much about money and finances, and most parents don't either. Most people learn (or don't learn) by trial and error along the way of life. These can be expensive lessons.

Develop your financial literacy along with your regular studies at school. You could do this as home work (see lesson #23). Learn about superannuation, insurance, depreciation, taxation, budgeting, borrowing, investment, compound interest, loans, deductions, assets, liabilities, shares, property, banking and retirement planning.

There are plenty of excellent books, magazines and websites that you can learn from, but beware of spruikers! If you know someone who is financially savvy, see if they will mentor you. The earlier you start the better!

What do I need to learn about financial matters?

Money and financial knowledge
is usually inherited
rather than taught,
more is the pity.

49 - Set limits: Say 'No'

You cannot do everything or please everybody. You don't have to. What you do need to do is work out what is OK for you and what is not, then clearly define those boundaries for yourself and others. Say 'No' to that extra drink, the unwanted puppy, unwelcome advances, unfair treatment, distasteful jokes, unreasonable requests, emotional blackmail or anything that you choose not to do. You don't need to offer a reason or an excuse. This is not about being rude or unhelpful or refusing to try new things. It is just stating clearly that you have boundaries that need to be respected. Don't compromise yourself.

What are my personal boundaries?

All that we are is the result of what we have thought.
The mind is everything.
What we think, we become.
Buddha

50 - Ending and beginning

Today marks the end of the term. It is also the beginning of the holidays. Every ending is a new beginning. When you lose something (or someone) it is not really the end … it is a new beginning. This can be hard to remember at times, but as you look back over your life you will see the truth of this simple idea. It is summed up in the famous phrase: The king is dead, long live the king!

What will I do over these holidays?

Life can seem like a dull, grey sentence
punctuated by bursts of colour
that we call holidays.

51 - Help out!

You are busy. Everyone is. Yes, you have study to do, but you can still help out. Wash the car. Wash the dishes. Cook a meal. Change the toilet roll. Walk the dog. Mow the lawn. Vacuum the house. Empty the dishwasher. Unload the shopping. Babysit. Clean your room. Chop some wood. Put the rubbish out. Bring the bin in. Sweep the verandah. Remove cobwebs. Recycle. Do some gardening. Hang out the washing. Light the fire. Set the table. Answer the phone. Bring in the mail. Put stuff away. Make your bed.

If you haven't done at least one of these things in the last few days it is time to step up. You may be surprised to find that you feel better about yourself when you do.

How can I help out today?

If you appreciate others helping you
the least you can do is help others too.
The time will come
when you will need help again.

52 - Move ahead

When I was learning to drive, my father told me to watch the road ahead and not to keep looking in the mirror at whoever was behind me. This was good advice for life too. You cannot change the past. What happened yesterday is history. Live today. Look to move forward in some way. Look to new opportunities and make a fresh start. Don't let who you were before stop you from being who you can be tomorrow. Move ahead and get on with living your own life.

What is ahead for me next?

*Knowing where we want to go
provides motivation and focus
and makes getting there more likely.*

53 - Make Time

There is always time to do what we really want to do – if we want it enough!

It is a case of priorities. How you use your time now is an indication of your priorities. Is there something else that you could or should be doing with your time? Study? Exercise? Reading? Working? Caring? Music? Planning? Volunteering? Playing?

When you want it enough you will make time to do it.

What could I make time for today?

Some days
feel longer than others.
How we use those 24 hours
can make all of the difference
to how we feel about the passing of time.

54 - Choose your battles

Sometimes we approach life with a single attitude or perspective. This is very limiting, even dangerous. If every issue makes us angry we could be looking at life through the wrong lenses. We need to learn what is appropriate in different circumstances and respond accordingly. Sometimes we run, sometimes we talk and sometimes we fight. Think about your choices. Reflect on your experiences. Consider some different options. Is there a better way?

What are the issues that I would fight for?

Water is amazing –
carving through huge rocks
and sprinkling gently on rose petals –
both soft and powerful.

55 - Look forward

When you are doing something hard or uninteresting, it helps to have something to look forward to. It may be the weekend, a television program, a party, concert, warm bath, holiday, trip or graduation. If you don't have anything to look forward to, a tedious job can seem endless and overwhelming.

Give yourself the gifts of hope, anticipation, expectation and delayed gratification. Plan something to look forward to.

What do I have to look forward to?

My raffle tickets
never win,
but somebody gets the prize
every time.

56 - Start now

Procrastination is one of the most common barriers to achievement and success.
I will do it when……………………………………………..
(insert time, event, excuse).

Do it now. Make a start. Stop putting it off. A job well started is a job half done. If you can't actually do it now, at least plan what needs to be done and draw up a schedule to do it. Write or enter it into your planner/diary. Doing nothing gets nothing done. Do something now!

What do I keep putting off doing?

Getting started is always the hardest part,
but it isn't as hard as it seems.
It just seems that way.

57 - Be Kind

There is a saying that goes: 'In a world where you can be anything, be kind.' This is good advice. The law of karma works here. What goes around comes around. Being kind is its own reward.

Kindness is not forgotten, even if it seems that it is not always appreciated or acknowledged. You can choose to make a difference. The world can be a better place because of you. We can all use a little kindness. Be kind.

How can I be kinder today?

*The best thing that we can do for ourselves
is to do something kind
for someone else.*

58 - Use your influence

Most of us are concerned about a whole range of big issues that we seem to have no control over. We want to stop global warming, achieve world peace and put an end to poverty, but we feel powerless to change these things. Worrying about things we cannot change is frustrating and time wasting. By focusing on doing what we can however, we gradually increase our sphere of influence and make a considerable contribution to improving those things that concern us most.

What can I do today to be part of the solution rather than the problem?

*Until we do what we can do,
we will never be able to change
the things that we can't change
yet ...*

59 - Be open to change

You may be right, but you can also be wrong. We don't start out in life knowing everything. Be open to new information and be prepared to change. Denying reality will not change the facts. Standing strong is admirable but being stubborn or remaining ignorant doesn't make any sense. Be open. Listen to advice, especially from those who have more experience and have your interests at heart. A change of belief, direction or attitude is not a weakness, but can be a sign of strength, intelligence and maturity.

What belief, direction or attitude may I need to change?

*We should always be open to change,
never settling for the status quo.
Leave that to statues.*

60 - Be grateful

On a cold winter's night, be aware of those without a warm bed or hot shower. As you sit in class, be aware of those who cannot access an education. As you enjoy your food, think of those who are hungry. When you are on holidays, think of those who have to work every day just to survive.

You have much to be thankful for.

Practise gratitude and appreciation each day.

What am I grateful for today?

*If there was a competition
to see who had the hardest life,
I would lose by a mile.*

61 - Get lucky

It is said: 'The harder you work the luckier you get'. There are a lot of similar sayings: 'Fortune favours the brave' and 'Success is dependent on effort' (Sophocles). We often say 'Good luck' to friends as they try to achieve something. We can increase our own luck by having a go. Whether it is winning a raffle or a lucrative scholarship, getting a job or a partner, starting a task or a journey, we will get luckier the more we practise, prepare and participate. A lucky colleague of mine often won staff raffles, but then he always bought a stack of tickets. You have to be in it to win it!

How can I improve my luck today?

*Luck is something you make for yourself,
then it follows you around
like a loyal puppy.*

62 - Speak kindly

You may not be able to change the world, but you can change the words that you speak. In fact, you are the only person who can do that. Speak kindly. Use positive words that build people up. Avoid coarse, ugly, abusive language. Speak warmly, honestly, pleasantly, assertively and gently. Be the kind of person that people like to hear from.

Who needs my kind words today?

What you say
can be a priceless treasure
or a costly burden.
It is entirely up to you.

63 - Be a good role model

We all have role models. People we look up to, admire and want to be more like. A good role model can inspire us and keep us on track.

Remember that as a senior student (older sibling, adult, teacher, parent), you are a role model too. Younger students, your peers and especially younger siblings look to you to be their example and guide. Being conscious of this, you can ensure that you are a good role model in all that you do or say, how you treat others, how you approach your work/studies and how you present and take care of yourself.

What kind of role model am I?

People are social by nature.
Most of what we know
we learn from each other.
Try to be a good teacher.

64 - Writers write

This was one of the best pieces of advice that I received as a writer. Writers write. It is no good saying that you want to write a book if you don't write. Watching television won't get it done. Nor will spending time on social media. Make the time. Find the time. Just do it.

What is it that you want to do? What do you want to be good at? Juggling? Speaking another language? Playing a musical instrument?

I have read that it takes about 10,000 hours to master a skill or area of knowledge, to become really good at it. That is roughly 417 days or 14 months if you do it full time. Most people take about ten years. The sooner you start the better.

What have I always wanted to be able to do or be good at?

Most of us have more potential than we realise.
We can do almost anything that we set our heart and mind to,
provided we are prepared to pay the price
in terms of time, sacrifice and effort invested.

65 - Have fun

Don't take yourself, or life, too seriously. I have a poster on my office door of an elephant under a waterfall. He looks very happy! The caption (usually attributed to Oscar Wilde) reads: 'Life is too important to be taken seriously'.
    Find ways to add some fun to your life. Learn to laugh at yourself. Collect jokes. Hang around with funny people. Wear costumes. Do things that you enjoy. Even playing games with little kids can be a great way to tap into the inner child and to keep things in perspective.

What can I do that is fun today?

*Just think how happy you'd be
if you lost everything you have right now –
and then got it back again.*
Anonymous

66 - Work smarter

There are numerous books, video clips and posters about how to work smarter. They include tips about goal setting, time management, paper-handling, running meetings and avoiding procrastination. Working harder for longer can solve some problems, but in the long run it makes more sense to work smarter, not harder. This is referred to as 'sharpening the saw'. How can you be more efficient, organised, focused and effective? Are your priorities clear to you? Is your workspace organised? Can someone else help to share the load? Do you know the traps that slow and distract you?

What is one way that I can work smarter today?

Make habits into allies
by evaluating and changing them from time to time.

67 - Choose your focus

We live in a complex world. There are so many things competing for our attention that we cannot possibly see or know everything. Under these circumstances we need to choose our focus. I choose to look at the positive, the beautiful, the hope-giving and awe-inspiring. These things are just as real as the sad, degrading, corrupt and outright evil aspects of life, but I have a choice.

You too can choose your perspective, your outlook, your focus. Our old school motto was 'Choose Life'. That seems like a good focus to me.

What do I tend to focus on in my life?

What we focus on grows,
be it a grudge or gratitude.
But we have choice.
We always have a choice.

68 - Learn acceptance

Some things are wrong. Very wrong. So wrong that they need to be changed. Some things just are. They won't change, at least not for now. It is nothing personal … it just is. Learning this simple lesson can save you untold unnecessary angst and frustration. Sometimes it is easier to change ourselves and our attitude, even if it is just for now. A little acceptance can go a long way.

What do I need to learn to accept more graciously?

Change what you can.
Deal with what you can't change.
Don't waste your life complaining.

69 - Write notes

In this digital age of social media likes and shares, it is still nice to get a handwritten note. With the popularity of Post-it notes this is also very easy.

A simple 'Thank you' or 'Thinking of you' can make a person's day. 'I love you', 'I miss you' and 'Have a nice day' with your name and some hugs and kisses added can be a nice surprise for someone special. Try to leave one note each day or week for the rest of the year.

Who can I surprise with a little note today?

*The habit of writing notes
is unusual in today's world,
but if anything,
this adds to its value
and importance.*

70 - Ask for help

Your parents, friends and teachers are not mind readers. If you need something, ask. If something really bothers you, tell someone. If you have an opinion or a problem, share it. If you don't know what to do, get assistance.

There is nothing to be gained by hoping that people will notice and work out what you want. You need to tell them or ask for help. This can be challenging at first, but it is worthwhile. The alternative can be frustrating for all concerned, so be honest and ask for what you need.

What do I really need today?

*They say that good things come to those who wait,
but they come more quickly
to those who know how to ask
for what they need.*

71 - Cultivate loyalty (even to strangers)

Don't talk about people behind their backs. Don't put other people down. Don't even listen to others backstabbing their friends, bosses, co-workers or family members. Walk away from this kind of negativity. Treat people with respect and kindness. Get a reputation for speaking well of others. Be loyal and trustworthy to friends, family and colleagues. If you treat people well, they will do the same for you. (Even if they don't – don't lower your standards!)

Who can I say something positive about today?

*It is so easy to get caught up in a gossip session,
but far more enjoyable
to share praise and compliments.*

72 - Invest in yourself

How do you spend your time, money and energy? A big chunk of your effort should be invested in yourself – your learning, your growth, your health and your development as a person. You are worth it! Investing in yourself is the best investment you can make. New knowledge, skills and experiences empower you to live a fuller, richer, wiser life.

How do I feel about investing in myself?

*You can afford to invest in yourself,
even when you have nothing else to invest,
and the returns last a lifetime.*

73 - Create networks

Talk to people. Lots of people. Teachers on duty. Friends of your parents. Neighbours watering their gardens. People on the train or bus. Friends of friends. Checkout operators. Everyone! Why? Because often it is not what you know, but who you know that counts in getting jobs and getting by in life. Building social networks gives you confidence in talking with others, enables you to meet amazing people, and teaches you life lessons that you will never get in the classroom.

How do I feel about talking to new people?

*Every person
has their own wisdom,
their own way of looking at life,
their own special knowledge
and gifts to share.*

74 - Make choices (and make them good!)

Love is a choice. Fitness is a choice. Working hard is a choice. Getting out of bed is a choice.

Success is all about making choices. Whatever success means for you, make choices and make it happen.

What choices have I made today?

Doing nothing is a choice,
but it is rarely the right one.

75 - Mark progress

This is the halfway mark of the year. How are you progressing? Do you need to work harder to achieve your goals or are you 'on pace' at this stage? It is good to use markers along the way to check your progress. Each week, month, term or semester is a time to review and reflect on how we are going. What am I pleased with so far? What do I need to change? What are my priorities?

What do I need to change today?

*Each milestone is significant,
marking progress on the journey,
encouraging us to keep moving forward.*

76 - Be still

Turn off the noise. Close the door. Take time to think, plan, reflect and dream. Do this for ten minutes each day. Listen to your thoughts. Listen to your heart. Let your mind wander. Whether you meditate or just sit or lie down, make some time each day to be still. Tap into your natural creativity and boost your productivity by doing nothing for a while. You may be surprised by the outcomes.

What do I need to change to find peace in my life?

*To be still
and do nothing
is often the something
that needs to be done.*

77 - Stay safe

You have your whole life ahead of you. There is so much to look forward to. Don't take unnecessary risks that may jeopardise your life. If you are driving, or learning how to, be careful. Wear safety equipment in workshop situations. Wear a helmet when riding a bike, horse or anything that you could crash with or fall off. Avoid illegal drugs and excessive alcohol. Check water depth before jumping or diving into water.

All things that you know already. All common sense. All ways that people have died or been severely injured. Friends I went to school with. Students I have taught. People I knew. Stop and think before you act!

What unnecessary risks do I take in my life?

Some risks are worth taking.
Some are not.
Learning the difference is important –
your life might depend on it.

78 - Admit mistakes

You will make mistakes. It is part of the human condition. Be prepared to say, 'Sorry'. Admit it when you make a mistake. Swallow your medicine. Take responsibility for your actions. Don't carry guilt, secrecy or regret. Be honest with yourself and with others. Learn humility. Build trust and integrity. Earn respect. Be real.

What mistakes have I made recently?

*It is human to make mistakes,
but we can learn and grow
from these lessons in humility.*

79 - Ask questions

Questions are powerful. They show that you are not just listening but thinking too. You can learn a lot from the answer to a good question. Don't be afraid to follow up with another question if you still don't understand. Keep asking. Persevere until you learn what you need to know.

What do I want to know more about today?

Those who have all of the answers haven't been asked all of the questions yet.

80 - Avoid predictions

Don't waste time second-guessing what is going to happen tomorrow, or any time in the future. It may never happen. The best predictor of the future is what we do in the present. We don't know how others will react, how our health will be impacted, what world events or natural disasters may or may not occur. Fear and worry can stop us from living life to the full. Avoid predictions. Build foundations, networks and relationships instead.

What can I do today?

Be thankful that you don't know the future.
It leaves more options open for you
and allows you to develop your imagination.

81 - Don't judge by school reports

A school report is a useful way to learn some things about a person, but it doesn't tell you much, so don't judge yourself (or others) by it. Thomas Edison reportedly failed at school. So did Richard Branson. Your success in life is not determined by your success at school. Good grades can give you more options in the short term and get you into a university course, but who you are and what you do with your other gifts are just as important for your ultimate sense of happiness and fulfilment – which are far better measures of success than a few grades in a few boxes.

What important things do my school reports NOT say about me?

*What can be measured
and written down briefly,
cannot possibly be a full and accurate summation
of any human being.*

82 - Live simply

You may have heard the saying: 'Live simply so that all may simply live'. How can you live more simply? What are the things that you can do without? How much waste does your lifestyle create?

You don't need a lot of things to be happy. You don't need to compete with or impress others by having the latest and greatest of everything ... the newest phone, the best clothes, the highest pay. Trying to keep up with (or pass) the Joneses is a recipe for disaster, not just for you, but for our planet too. A simple, joyful life of enough is enough.

How much is enough for me?

There is a beauty in simplicity
that belongs to but a few.
These and only these
are good enough for you.

83 - Give cheerfully

Everyone loves a cheerful giver, or so the saying goes. The truth is that giving is good for us. Be it time or money or some special gift that we have (e.g. singing or IT skills), the world is a better place when we learn how to give. It seems counter-intuitive, but most financial advice courses include a section on giving or gifting money to others. It not only helps them, but it makes us feel good too, AND it helps us to develop a healthy relationship with money, or whatever our gift is. Try it for yourself and see!

What do I have to give today?

*What we cannot give away
owns us
more than we own it!*

84 - Allow gaps

Do not fill your life up with the doing of things or imagine that you can switch instantly from one task to another. You need spaces to transition. It takes time to travel in mind and body from one task to another, one activity to another. Give yourself time and space. Schedule gaps between things. Give yourself time to unwind, disentangle, relax and reset. In work and in relationships, exercise and travel, leave some gaps between events.

How long do I realistically need between activities?

*Time is the mortar
between the bricks of life.
The spaces
are a part of the structure too.*

85 - Offer Praise Often

Whenever you catch someone doing the right thing, praise them. Become a good-finder. Look for goodness in others and acknowledge it. Be quick to show gratitude. Say, 'Thank You', 'I appreciate your effort', or 'You did that well'.

The world is a much better place for all of us when we see and acknowledge the good in each other.

(PS Don't forget to appreciate your own good points too!)

What do others compliment me for?

You can't 'make' other people happy,
but who you are and what you say
can make a significant and positive difference
to the quality and enjoyment of another person's life.

86 - Get back up

Things will go wrong. There will be roadblocks and obstacles in your life. Relationships will fail. People will die. You will get sick or hurt, often at inconvenient times. These challenges can knock you down, but you need to get back up, start again and keep going. Find another way. As one door closes, another one opens. It happens over and over again. Learn from the experience. Take a deep breath. Move in a different direction. You are a better person each time you face and deal with a new challenge.

What have I learned from the challenges that I have faced in my life?

*A life without challenges
is about as satisfying as a scoreless draw in a soccer match.*

87 - Be thankful

If you have this book and you can read then you already have much to be thankful for. Make a list of your gifts: You can read. You have a home. A bed. A family. You can see. You can write. You can get an education. You have access to medical care. Perhaps you are learning to drive. You might have a pet, or a job ... or you could get one. You have food, fresh air, clean water to drink, access to technology and friends. There are so many things that we have and take for granted every day. Noticing them and being thankful adds to our quality of life.

What do I have to be thankful for?

We are not expected to start with nothing.
We already have more gifts and opportunities than we are aware of.

88 - Don't whinge

We live in an imperfect world. If you don't like something – change it! Do some research. Form a committee. Explore the options. Submit a proposal. Set up an alternative. Start a petition. Do something constructive to bring about the change that is needed. If you need inspiration, google 'Ryan's Well'.

If you can't change it, or you can't be bothered, don't whinge. That's not going to help anyone. Focus on what you can do, not what you can't.

What do I want to change today?

*You can achieve
a lot more than you realise,
but you have to do it
before you know that this is true.*

89 - Look inside

I love books, but I rarely buy them new. Garage sales and Op shops are great sources of good books at a reasonable price – usually only one or two dollars. The covers can be a bit scruffy, the edges may be aged, corners bent, and the inscription written for someone else, but those things don't matter. It is what is inside that matters; the words and the story. The best books are often the most worn and well used.

People can be like this. Life takes its toll on everyone. Age wearies and wears people down. Work and stress leave their mark, but the person is what counts. Their story is important. Their experience is valuable. Don't judge a book by its cover. Get to know the person behind the façade. You may uncover a hidden treasure!

Who have I judged without getting to know them?

*I keep getting surprised
by how much I don't know
about the people in my life.*

90 - Learn first aid

There are a few life skills everyone should have. Being able to do first aid is one of them. Whether you are babysitting, camping, partying, playing sport or working, you never know when you may need to use first aid skills or knowledge. Being able to resuscitate a loved one or help a total stranger is a blessing. There are plenty of short courses out there. Having this qualification on your CV looks good, but being able to save a life, or at least prevent an unnecessary death is invaluable. Do it!

When am I most likely to wish I knew first aid?

*Being able to help another person
is a gift that you give yourself,
a source of blessing and good karma.*

91 - Learn from mistakes

Unless you do nothing, you will make mistakes. We all do. The important thing is to learn from them. Learn what to not do or say or try again, and then move on.

Too many people hold on to their mistakes and measure their worth by their failures. Instead, fix up what you can, forgive yourself and others, then forge ahead. Life is so much more than our mistakes. Success is built on action, not regret. Build a bridge!

What did you learn from your last mistake?

*We learn by doing
and we often get it wrong,
but that is not all of the story.*

92 - Welcome rain

Rain can seem like a painful inconvenience, but welcome it anyway! It is a free gift, our source of life. Rain waters the earth and the plants that we eat. It cleans the air and settles the dust. It fills our dams, lakes, rivers and aquifers so that we have water to drink, wash and play with. The bottom line is: you can't stop the rain, so you might as well enjoy it – and it is beneficial to you!

How can I respond more positively to weather extremes?

*Each season
brings its own blessings
and the changing weather
saves us from boredom
and predictability.*

93 - Don't be a victim

The world is full of good people. Kind, helpful, loving people. But there are some who are damaged or disturbed, sometimes violent and dangerous. Don't let them spoil your life. If you are being hit, bullied or mistreated in any way, get out and get help. If you want to try and help the perpetrator, then get back-up. Don't let yourself become isolated, vulnerable or co-dependent. Let bullies know that you are not alone, that you have support and back-up. Don't let them manipulate or fool you. Don't be a victim. You deserve better and they need to know that you have firm boundaries that cannot be crossed!

Who does not treat me with the respect that I deserve?

*If they hit you once
it is too often.
They will do it again.
Get out while you can.*

94 - Develop good habits

Most of what we do each day is habitual. We don't really think about it consciously, we just do it. Over time we develop all kinds of habits. The way we dress or eat or the route we take to school or work is virtually automatic. But some habits are better than others. Procrastinating, swearing, eating junk food and making excuses can become habits too.

Researchers say it takes about four weeks to develop a new habit. If you know what your bad habits are, you can gradually work at replacing them with good habits that will help you to achieve your goals, be healthier and feel better about your life.

What good habits do I want to develop?

*Habits can be the best of friends
or the worst of enemies,
but they don't have to stay that way.
As hard as it may be,
we can change our habits.*

95 - Build something

Every building started off as an idea. Someone had a dream, a vision, a plan. Weeks, months, or even years of planning and refinement took place before the first foundations were poured and the first stone or brick was laid. Gradually the structure took shape and rose. People moved in and life flowed through the building.

What are you building? What plan do you have? Who will 'inhabit' your dreams? Who will you shelter or employ or meet along the way?

What kind of foundations am I building with my life?

There is a great joy in making something,
in shaping and forming
a piece of plasticine,
or a garden,
or a life.

96 - Take breaks

Give yourself permission to take breaks. To have time out. To rest and recover and reset. There is more to life than endless hurry and bustle. You want to make the most of your life, and sometimes that means contemplating a flower or a sunset or watching some mindless TV. Do whatever enables you to do what needs to be done for the rest of the time.

How do I take breaks from my work?

Breaks are the punctuation that puts order and sense into the busy jumble of life.

97 - Go first

Nothing gets done until someone makes the first move. Starting a job, asking a question, trying a new process, going in a new direction, making a suggestion. Someone has to do it.

Be that someone. Be a catalyst. Dare to have a go. Set the tone. Be an example. Take a risk. You won't always be right, but you will start the process that leads to success and achievement ... and you will learn from the experience.

What can I start doing today?

Going first is risky.
You may not get it right,
but it is not wrong to have a go.

98 - Don't give up

History is full of stories of people who finally succeeded after many setbacks, injuries, hardships, rejections and failures. The one thing that they all have in common is that they didn't give up. We never hear about the people who stopped trying. We only know about those who kept on going, persevering in the face of adversity. Be one of them. Don't give up!

What is something that I am still trying to do?

Don't be surprised when things don't go according to plan.
That is a part of life.
More importantly, don't be put off by this.
Stick to your process and work towards your goals.

99 - Walk more

Walking 10,000 steps a day has become a popular target for those with wearable devices. Some do even more than this. The secret is to make walking part of your life rather than seeing it as another exercise activity to be done. Making the effort to walk is one of the best choices that you can make for your health. Walk to a nearby office instead of sending an email. Walk up the stairs instead of taking the lift or escalator. Walk to the local shop or school or library. Walk down the street to catch a bus or visit a friend. Walk around the golf course instead of using a buggy. Walk outside to check the weather or to look at the moon. Our bodies were made to move. Walk more today.

Where will I start walking to today?

*I don't mind
if you walk ahead of me,
behind me or beside me
as long as we are walking
in the same direction.*

100 - Review and reset

Two terms down. One to go. How is it going so far? Seriously. What is working for you? What needs adjustment?

Just as a car needs to be serviced, maintained and retuned, our lives need regular reviews, adjustments and check-ups. Medical and dental checks. Skin checks. Finances and budget tracking. Exercise, diet, relationships, study, work – all need to be checked and reviewed to see if they are heading in the right direction or need some kind of action to improve them.

The end of the term is a good time to do this. So is the beginning of term … or any other day of your life!

How am I really travelling at present?

Starting off in the right direction
is a good way to start,
but no guarantee
of getting to where you want to go.

101 - New beginnings

Each new day is a new beginning. As this new term gets underway, what new things are you looking forward to? What changes are you going to make? What are your goals and expectations? Don't just let one day roll into another without touching base with your aims and hopes for the future. Like a wedding anniversary, each new day or week or term marks our progress along the way to where we want to go, to how we want to be and to what we want to achieve. Do something to mark this day and to make it memorable. This is the first day of the rest of your life – live it!

What can I do today to start this term off well?

*Starting in the right way
makes the whole journey easier.*

102 - Make Order

Do you lose things like keys, glasses, pens, watches, phones or tickets? Do you put things down and then forget where you put them? Do you waste time frantically searching for things when you are in a hurry to go out or get somewhere?

Many people do, but you can change this. Developing order, system and regular habits will help. As the proverbial saying goes: A place for everything and everything in its place. Put a key-hook or box or bowl inside the door – and USE IT! Place glasses, watches or your phone in the same place each time you put them down … or don't put them down. Have a place (like the Tickler File in Life Lesson #6) for keeping tickets, bills and paperwork. Have a pen or stationery drawer. Get spare glasses if you need to use them in more than one place and keep them in the car or at work.

Using good habits and strategies like these can save a lot of time and frustration.

What new organisational habit can I start today?

You will find it
where you left it
if you know
where you left it!

103 - Do care

Saying, 'I don't care' is often a sign of ignorance, laziness or cruelty. If you know about a person in need or an issue that requires action, then not caring is not an option. You may be too busy to help out right now, have problems of your own or not know what to do, but sometimes just listening or being aware can be a response in itself. At least be interested. Make an effort to know what the problem is so that you can make an informed response or alert others about the situation.

Imagine if you were in real need and someone couldn't even be bothered finding out about your situation. Being deliberately ignored feels worse than the actual hardship or problem.

The measure of a person is how we treat our fellow human beings. Do care!

Who/What do I want to care more about?

*Being aware
shows you care,
even if
that is all you can do
for now.*

104 - Find good

There is much in the world that is bad. We can see it on TV or any news app.

There is also much in the world that is good. We can hear it and see it all around us if we make the effort to look. Every cloud has a silver lining and there is more than enough good news out there for everyone to share.

Just having the ability to see, touch, hear, taste and feel is good. Look for the good and you will find it. See the beautiful, the heroic, the kind, the creative, the quirky, the healthy, the helpful and the courageous. See the little things: the smiles, laughter, warmth, humour, flowers, colours, stars and sunsets.

What good can I find in my life today?

*So much good
is out there too.
If you look,
you will find
this is true.*

105 - No excuses

Excuses are not very helpful. They are a way of avoiding responsibility for our own lives and actions. Growing up means accepting responsibility. If you find yourself repeatedly making excuses for being late, not handing work in on time or forgetting promises or appointments, then it is time to take a good hard look at yourself. What do you need to change about your attitude, record keeping, time management or decision making processes? It is up to you. Don't blame others for things that you can control and change.

What excuses do I use for not doing things?

*An excuse
is not an acceptable explanation.
It prevents us from taking responsibility for ourselves.*

106 - Attend funerals

If a close friend or relative or family friend dies, go to their funeral. Apart from showing respect for the person and giving support to their loved ones, funerals can be powerful lessons in life and perspective. They remind us of our own mortality. They give us an insight into what is valued and important in life. They often help us to see another side of a person we may have judged or categorized unfairly.

Funerals prompt us to put life into perspective and provide us with a pause for reflection and reconnection with our own life, purpose and meaning.

What is one thing that I would love to do before I die?

There is almost always
a baby at a funeral.
Like the bookends of life:
One who dies,
One who cries.

107 - Take charge

One very important lesson that I have learnt was that I am 100% responsible for my own behaviour. As a teacher, my students don't make me angry or sad or disappointed or happy. I am responsible for my own life, my moods, my reactions and my choices. I can blame and complain as much as I like, but it all comes back to me. What I choose to say, or think, is what shapes my experience of life, not the other way around.

The same is true of you. You too are 100% responsible for your behaviour. No blame. No excuses. No complaints. What are YOU going to do about it?

In what ways have I been responsible today?

I can do it ... I can do it ... I can do it!
Like a mantra,
this self-fulfilling prophecy
is one of the most powerful lessons
we can learn.

108 - Be Happy

So often we look for happiness in the wrong places. We wait expectantly for that magical day or thing or person that will make us happy, but it always seems to be out of reach. In reality, being happy is more about a choice that we make rather than something that we have to work towards or wait for. We can choose to be happy each day if that is what we want. Being happy makes us happy. That is all we need. We can also share our happiness with others. There is plenty to go around. You are given a choice. Being happy is up to you.

How happy do I want to be today?

We spend so much time yearning for that special item
that will finally make us happy,
that we don't take the time to look around
and discover that we already are.
Anonymous

109 - Bad days happen

Bad days happen to everyone. Things go wrong. Accidents occur. You forget to do something. You lose something or someone important. All of the traffic lights are red. You are late for an appointment. You drop your phone and smash the screen. You miss the bus. It is not your lucky day. Everything seems to be working against you.

Don't take it personally. Everyone has bad days. There is no big conspiracy. Get over it and get on with life. Do what needs to be done to get through and repair the damage.

Tomorrow is another day. Good days happen too. Life goes on …

How do I respond to things going wrong in my life?

*You can't see much
from the middle of a bad day.
Better to have a good sleep
and look with fresh eyes in the morning.*

110 - Take Breaks II

Working for too long at one time is not effective. For most people, 40 minutes is the optimal period to focus on one task. Set a timer and see how you go. Then you should have a short break.

Take a walk or have a short nap. Do a few exercises. Enjoy a drink or a snack. Talk to a family member or friend. Walk the dog. Play with a younger sibling. Read for pleasure. Take a shower or have a dip in the pool. Daydream. Play music. Meditate.

You'll go back to the next task refreshed and re-energised.

What will I gain by taking short breaks?

*A short break
is like a mini-holiday
that your brain looks forward to
and returns from refreshed and revitalised.*

111 - Start your Super

All of the smart investment advisors promote the benefits of superannuation, and most of them say that the earlier you start the better. This is because of the power of compound interest over time.

If you have a part time job and you or your parents can put some money into a low fee superannuation scheme, you will be a step ahead of most of the population come retirement time. (You may also be able to take advantage of the Australian government's co-contribution scheme for lower paid workers to get extra benefits.)

How much can I afford to put into superannuation now?

*The time to do something about your superannuation
is before you need it.
By the time that you need it,
it is too late.*

112 - Be nice

'Nice' is one of those four letter words that English teachers urge us to avoid when writing about a character. It is too bland they say. Be more creative. Describe them as generous or charitable or appealing instead. But being nice is still something worth doing. It may mean different things to different people, but most of us have a general idea of what it means to be nice and can choose to act that way if we want to. Being nice is better than the alternative.

How can I be a nicer person today?

Being nice or kind or good
means doing the things that you should.
People will notice and you will find
that others are also good or nice or kind.

113 - Use your manners

One way of being nice, showing gratitude, and just getting along with other people, is to use your manners. Some people think that manners are old-fashioned or that you have to show respect to earn respect, but good manners simply show that we are decent human beings who recognise and appreciate each other and what we do. 'Please' and 'thank you' are such important words, as are 'I am sorry' and 'excuse me' and 'may I'. If we forget our manners, we forget our humanity. We are denying a very important part of who we are in relationship to one another. These magic words that we learn in kindergarten are just as important in high school, at home, at university or in a workplace.

Where can I use better manners today?

Manners are not out-dated.
Their importance cannot be over-stated.

114 - Write goals

Some lessons are so important that they are worth repeating. Writing your goals is one of them. The evidence shows that writing down your goals makes a significant positive difference to how you live your life. Having a clear focus and a goal that you can see before you makes it easier to get started and to keep going each day.

What is my main goal today?

*Writing goals is something I do
and I have achieved quite a few.
It's true there is a long list still
of things I haven't done, but will.
I think that it is quite okay
to save them for another day.*

115 - Make a difference

You can't solve all of the world's problems, but you can still make a difference. Small daily actions can make the world of difference to the people around you, and the ripple effect that you create may produce amazing results. Simply smiling more or remembering someone's name could do it.

You only fail when you fail to do what you can. Make the effort to make a positive difference today.

How can I begin to make a positive difference today?

What you do does make a difference.
Don't be fooled or overwhelmed by bad news —
you have more power and influence than you realise.

116 - Try something new

Everything that you do now was once new for you. From first steps to first kiss, there is a first time for everything. Sometimes it is great, and you keep doing it, or it isn't, and you learn from the experience. Either way, you will never, never know until you give it a go. Try a new author, a new colour, a new way to cut your toast, a new kind of tea, a new food or drink, a new hairstyle, a new restaurant, a new pen, a new dentist, a new sport, a new musical instrument, a new language, a new profile picture, a new routine or a new habit. Perhaps trying new things could be your new habit!

What is something new that I could try?

*New things
are like treasures
waiting to be discovered.*

117 - Parenting 101

You're not ready for this yet. I get that. But many of you will be parents one day. What have you learned about parenting? What are the good things that your parents do that you would like to do as a parent one day? What things would you change? What can you learn by observing parents on TV, the parents of your friends and other people that you know?

Parenting is one of the most important things that you will ever do if you choose to do so, so it makes sense to give it some thought in advance and to learn as much as you can along the way.

What have I learned about parenting in my life so far?

Our children learn from us.
We owe it to them to learn as much as we can
about how to be good parents, examples and role models,
so that we can do a good job when our turn comes.

118 - Eat natural

Part of being healthy is eating healthy. The less processed a food is the healthier it is. You know this! Whenever you have a choice, choose natural. Eat fruit instead of drinking juice. Snack on vegetables of nuts rather than biscuits, cake or chips. Try different fruits and enjoy the variety of tastes and textures. Drink water instead of soft drink or so-called 'power drinks'. Snack on carrots sticks, capsicum or mushrooms. Take a fruit platter to a party instead of a packet of mixed pastries. What you put into your body makes a big difference over a lifetime ... why not make it a positive difference?

What healthy eating choice have I made recently?

*Healthy eating habits
benefit the mind,
the body
and the planet.*

119 - Push yourself

I am not suggesting that you stress or hurt yourself by doing too much, but most of us don't know our limits because we never even get near to them. We stay well within our comfort zone and do enough to get by, but no more.

Sometimes it is good to push ourselves. To compete with a friend or peer, to race against the clock or calendar, or simply to strive more than usual to get better results more quickly. In times of crisis, people amaze themselves by coping better than they expected by finding hidden reserves of strength or patience that they never even knew they had. With more effort, you might amaze yourself too and discover new levels of performance and achievement.

How can I push myself this week?

*Knowing our limits is good for our self-esteem.
It gives us a realistic understanding of what we can and can't do,
helps us to set appropriate boundaries,
to say 'Yes' and 'No' with clarity
and to make space for some 'maybe I can'.*

120 - Expect the unexpected

I love to write goals and make plans for the future and feel that I have some control over my life, but often things don't turn out as expected. A visit from an old friend, an injury or illness, a natural disaster, a distress call, a divorce, a sick child or parent or friend, a lotto win or a major world event like September 11 can change your plans or even shake the whole world. This is NOT a reason to stop planning and setting goals, just don't be surprised when the unexpected leads to a change from time to time. It may even lead to an opportunity you hadn't planned on.

How did I deal with the last unexpected event in my life?

*Life would be pretty boring or scary
if we could predict everything that was going to happen,
but we can't, so enjoy the ride!*

121 - Share it

Parents often tell us to share with our siblings or friends, but we shouldn't stop there. Sharing can make our whole lives feel much better.

Whether it is food, space, a confidence, time, money, ideas, conversation or holidays, sharing can add to the enjoyment and quality of life. People are also more likely to share with us if we share with them. This could be a random act of kindness, the start of a new friendship or a way of cementing an existing relationship. You could begin by sharing this idea now.

What could I share with someone today?

*Sharing takes us out of ourselves,
encourages interaction and builds trust.
Start small and see what happens.*

122 - Enjoy lunch

So often lunch is a rushed break between periods of work. Meetings can even be scheduled during lunch breaks as if stopping to eat is of secondary importance. Instead, make lunch a special treat. Find a peaceful place where you can sit in comfort and enjoy your food. Take time to savour the taste of your food. Chew slowly. Have something different to eat each day. Go out to a garden or park to eat if the weather is suitable. Go for a short walk after you have eaten. Eat with a friend or make some space for yourself. Close your eyes for a few moments. Make your lunch break a mini holiday.

How could I make my lunch special today?

*A good lunch break
is like a mini holiday,
it refreshes and reinvigorates.*

123 - Accept less than perfect

As a perfectionist, I have spent many hours of my life trying to do things just right, to make them perfect. A wise colleague pointed out that most people don't notice or care about the little details I fuss about. Sometimes 'good enough' is good enough. Trying to do everything perfectly is a recipe for stress and frustration. It can't be done! Learning to lower your standards in some areas can make you easier to live with and perhaps help you to accept when others don't meet the standards you might be expecting from them.

What can I do less perfectly and still feel okay about?

*Trying to be perfect
means not accepting my humanity –
being intolerant of aspects of my life
that are beyond my control.*

124 - Aim high

This lesson is about self-belief. So often we undersell ourselves. We don't appreciate our true value. Our giftedness. Our power. Having big dreams to aim for gives us hope. It creates an expectation. It gives us a goal to work towards and the motivation to make a difference. It opens our eyes to opportunities that we might otherwise pass by without even noticing.

How do we do this? One way is to imagine what it is that we would be most disappointed about if we did NOT achieve it ... then double it or aim higher! Write down your dreams today and set your sights on achieving them ... step by step, day by day. You may surprise yourself with what is possible.

What is the big dream that most inspires and motivates me?

*The greater danger for most of us
is not that we aim too high and we miss it,
but that we aim too low
and we reach it.*
Michelangelo

125 - Trust your gut

Our society places great emphasis on science and reason, evidence and data. These are good and useful, even sensible most of the time, but our own intuition, our 'gut feeling', about something is also important and shouldn't be ignored. This is especially true in relationships and lifestyle decisions. Recent research backs this up, showing that our gut is much more than a food processing factory. Learn to listen to your own deep feelings and to follow what your gut instinct is telling you to do … or at least check it out, just in case. Lives have been saved, fortunes made, and great friendships built by people responding to a 'gut feeling'. Trust your intuition.

What is my gut feeling at the moment?

*It takes guts
to trust your gut,
but what is right for you
should feel right to you.*

126 - Review your day

Every day is a little bit different. It is also a gift of time for us to use. A blessing to be counted or a cross to be carried. Take a few moments at the end of each day to review the events of that day. What are you thankful for? What did you learn? How could you have made the day better? You may like to record some of these things in a journal to see if there are any patterns emerging or changes that you need to make. Ultimately, we live one day at a time. Make the most of each day by taking the time to learn its lessons.

How was this day for me?

This day will not be repeated.
No day is.
I need to learn this.

127 - Learn some basics

This lesson could also be called: 'How to avoid sounding stupid'. There are a number of basic terms and ideas that are commonly used and widely accepted, but rarely understood. Many of my students insist that they believe in the 'Big Bang', but they know nothing about it. They can't tell me when it occurred, who developed the theory, what times and temperatures were involved or what evidence there is to support it.

Everyone has heard of Einstein's $e = mc^2$, but most people don't know what the letters stand for or what it means. Quantum physics and relativity are a bit harder to understand, but some knowledge of the uncertainty principle, the dual nature of light and the sheer enormity of the distance travelled in a light year are worth knowing something about. The same is true for the theory of evolution and a basic understanding of history, religions and geography. Having a basic grasp of geometric progression and compound interest are also worthwhile.

You are entitled to your own opinions, but do your research and try to develop some understanding of what it is that you believe and why.

What do I need to learn more about?

*The Big Bang
is one of the most widely held
and least understood
ideas of science.*

128 - Don't take it personally

Have you ever been so caught up in your own thoughts that you accidentally bumped into another person, or walked straight past a good friend without being able to remember their name? Or has another person done this to you? It was probably just an accident. Often we assume that someone else has done something TO us, when in fact it has nothing to do with us at all – we just happen to be in the wrong place at the wrong time. A lot of life is like this. It just happens – and we happen to be a part of it. There is no conspiracy against us. People do their own things for their own reasons, just as we do too. Even when it seems personal, it is often more about them than you. Let it go.

What should I stop taking personally?

*Most of the time
people don't think about us
as much as we think they do.
They are too busy thinking about themselves.*

129 - Get your passport

When you turn eighteen, go online and apply for a passport if you don't already have one. You may not intend travelling anytime soon, but your passport won't expire for ten years and it is useful as proof of your identity. More than this, having one means that you can be ready to go if an unexpected opportunity arises: a prize, a job offer, a surprise gift, an invitation, a bargain deal or a spur of the moment getaway.

Having this potential may also open your mind to see opportunities that you might otherwise miss out on.

Where would I like to travel to if given the choice?

*A passport
is more than a form of ID.
It is a ticket
that turns a chance
into an adventure.*

130 - Slow down

In a car, or in life generally, most of us are rushing around like there is no tomorrow. Sadly, for some people this is true, but most of us are just rushing without really thinking about it.

Slowing down in a car can save fuel, reduce the risk of an accident or serious injury and make driving less stressful. It also saves wear and tear on the car and makes the roads safer for others.

Slowing down in life also lowers stress levels, reduces mistakes and gives us time to smell the roses and enjoy the journey.

In what ways can I slow down today?

*Accepting that we can never get it all done
no matter how fast we go
enables us to slow down
without the fear of missing out.*

131 - Don't keep score

There are always lots of little jobs to be done at home, at work and at school. Ideally these jobs would be shared around equally, and everyone would take their turn. This is rarely true, however. You may be the only one who turns off the lights, brings in the rubbish bin, feeds the cat, cleans the car, locks the door, collects the mail, puts the milk back into the fridge, remembers the anniversary, does the shopping or makes the lunches. (NB I am not talking about the situation where you do ALL of the jobs for everyone else ALL of the time without any reciprocal benefits or payment– that is unfair). In truth, you have probably benefited from a whole lot of other people including parents, teachers, coaches, colleagues and friends doing little things like this for you over many years. Keeping score doesn't help anyone. It creates resentment or leads to a clumsy barter economy that is no basis for a proper relationship built on contribution and mutual respect. How do you measure the value of a hug, a smile or a song? What value love? Some things cannot and should not be tallied. If a job needs doing and you can do it, then do it!

What can I do to contribute today?

What can be measured
isn't that important.
What is important
is hard to measure.

132 - Get up earlier

You don't have to get up at a ridiculous time or while it is still dark, but most successful people make the most of the start of the day. Studies also suggest that getting up at a regular time is a healthy sleep habit to develop too.

Note – you still need to get enough sleep, but if you get up one hour before your peers, family or competitors, you get a great head start every day, and over a year that adds up to an extra fifteen days in which to study, meditate, work, think, play or exercise.

This is the time that I use to write or run, do a bit of quiet gardening or just to enjoy some personal space and plan my day. As soon as you wake up, get out of bed and see what a difference it makes.

How could I spend an extra hour each morning?

I am a morning person.
It is the best part of the day.
I hate to lay in bed awake –
I want to get up and get doing.

133 - Be a blessing

You can be a blessing or a curse. It is up to you. Blessing someone may be as simple as calling them by name, noticing when they are tired, doing some small act of kindness. It takes an effort of attitude and action, but it makes the world of difference to our experience of life. By looking for opportunities and choosing to care enough one can transform relationships, lift and inspire others and see the world as a place in which you have a role to play and a difference to make. Be a blessing.

How can I be a blessing for someone today?

*A life filled with blessing others
is not a guarantee of good karma,
but it will make you
more friends than enemies.*

134 - Exercise regularly

If there were only two habits I could promote for all of my students, family members and acquaintances, they would be reading (see Life Lesson #18) and exercise. Both are wonderful gifts to self.

Exercise and fitness benefit us along every step of our life journey and can extend the length and quality of that journey. Exercise is the best antidote to stress and depression, a great booster of self-esteem and confidence, a protection against many common ailments and a source of joy and unusual opportunities. It is available in a wide variety of forms and can be shaped to fit almost any lifestyle or personality type. Being fit for life is not compulsory, but it is well worth the effort and investment involved and continues to pay dividends year after year.

What form of exercise do I enjoy the most?

It is not just a matter of using it or losing it.
It is a deeper, more basic truth
that we can only learn through experience.

135 - Write by Hand

I don't mean to type or enter into your digital device. I am writing about writing – by hand! Despite living in a digital world, there are still times when a written note or card is more convenient, appropriate or meaningful. Reading and writing are still useful basic skills that are worth developing. Writing legibly is also something worth working on. Whether you are making a shopping list or writing a love letter, being able to write clearly and personally is useful. It is cheap and easy and even necessary in many situations.

How could I improve my handwriting?

*A handwritten message of thanks
or an expression of affection
conveys more than just words.
It is a personal touch
that goes deeper and lasts longer.*

136 - Never fail

This doesn't mean that you will succeed at everything you try first time around. What it does mean is that you change the way you think about the experience. Keep trying to do new and sometimes hard things even if they don't work out as hoped. We often learn more from so-called 'failures' than from what comes easily to us. As a result, we never fail as long as we grow from the experience and try again.

Labelling ourselves as 'a failure' is not very helpful. It could stop us from making the most of future opportunities too. Better to never fail but keep learning!

What would I try today if I knew that I could not fail?

*Failure is just a name for experiences
that didn't turn out as we had hoped.
It is not a permanent
or on-going condition.*

137 - Go green

This is about the environment and it is IMPORTANT! The future of the human race depends on all of us doing the right thing to care for the Earth and its resources. Air and water are essential for survival, but we want far more than just survival. We want a good quality of life for ourselves and for future generations. The mantra of 'reduce, re-use and recycle' can be applied to many aspects of our lives to ensure a sustainable and healthy future for us and our planet. Keep informed about what needs to be done and why AND take action to make a difference. What you do does matter and reducing your environmental footprint is an essential step. Your example can also inspire and motivate others to do the right thing too.

How can I be greener today?

All of my hopes and dreams
and wonderful schemes
are worthless
if I don't have clean air and water,
or a healthy environment
to live them out in.

138 - Join a group

Being part of a group widens your horizons, helps to develop social skills and enables you to express yourself in what is usually a supportive and encouraging environment. It doesn't matter which group it is or what they do as long as it is beneficial: a sporting or volunteer group, theatre arts or martial arts, moto-cross or music, SES or a book club, church youth or local naturalists.

If there isn't a group to cater for your particular interests then start a group of your own!

What kind of group would I like to join or create?

Being part of a group
helps us to feel needed and wanted,
while teaching us valuable lessons
about diversity, compromise, creativity and cooperation.

139 - Remember to play

As we get older it is easy to forget the joy of playing. We become more 'mature' and 'sensible' and 'serious', but we often lose touch with the child within and forget how to have fun and enjoy ourselves.

We are not talking organised sport or competition here. This is 'down on your hands and knees and using your imagination' stuff. This is making sandcastles, blowing bubbles, tickling and pretending. If you have younger siblings or neighbours or friends or family with young children then join in their games and rediscover the joy of being a child and living in the moment.

Perhaps you could include some traditional games in your next birthday party.

How could I introduce more play into my life?

Playing takes us back to a simpler time –
free of worries,
always now,
where for a little while
nothing else matters.

140 - Bite your tongue

OK – so don't take this literally, but this old saying means that we should stop and think before we say something. This is especially true of negative comments or criticism.

The old test was: Is it true? Is it necessary? Is it kind? If your answer to any of these questions is 'No' then you are probably better off NOT saying it. Think of the feelings of the other person. How do you feel when you are criticised? Don't inflict this pain on others. Bite your tongue, be more compassionate and try to be the better person.

Remember too that what we are most critical of in others, is often a reflection of some aspect of ourselves that we find hard to accept or express. Perhaps we need to examine this and make some changes to ourselves instead of projecting it onto others.

What is it that others do that I am most critical of?

*Negative comments
are like a barbed hook
that we cannot take back
without causing harm.*

141 - Love yourself

The principle of loving your neighbour as you love yourself or doing unto others as you want them to do to you, is almost universally known and accepted. Most belief systems have some variation of this maxim as a basic teaching. The problem is that the focus is often on doing good things for the neighbour or other while ignoring the very real need to love and be good to ourselves.

How do we love and accept ourselves? Do we look at ourselves with loving kindness? How do we look at our choices, our bodies and our contributions? Do we accept our flaws and limitations? Do we give ourselves second chances? Can we forgive ourselves?

It is good to love our neighbour, but we need to love ourselves first or we will not have the energy, patience or reserves to love others.

How can I love myself more today?

It is OK to be OK with who we are.
The measure that we use for our own value
is the same one that we will use for our neighbour.

142 - Keep improving

Even if you are pretty good at doing something, you can usually improve. This is true for driving a car, writing an essay, executing a golf swing or developing a new recipe. Most inventions and developments of any sort are the result of trying to improve something or to do it better. Our first attempt at anything is rarely the best that we can do. Our first steps may have thrilled our proud parents, but we got a lot better at walking with time and practise. The same is true of most of the things that we do. We can get better! We can improve.

What do I want to improve at today?

*Improvement
is always possible
because nobody is perfect.*

143 - Celebrate special days

Holidays, birthdays, public holidays, anniversaries and feast days (like St Patrick's Day) are all worth marking or celebrating in some way. These days commemorate people and events that have made a significant difference to a person, a family, a country or the world.

The least that we can do is acknowledge this. A card, a message, a ritual act, a gift or offering may be appropriate. You may like to develop some individual ways of marking days of importance by wearing themed clothes, visiting a particular person or place, preparing special food or making a personal gift.

What is the next special day on my calendar?

*Special days of celebration and remembrance
make all of the other 'ordinary' days worth living.*

144 - Do what you can

One of the most overused quotes in the life-coaching and self-help repertoire is: 'Do what you can, with what you have, where you are'. This is usually attributed to Theodore Roosevelt and the reason that it is overused is because it is so true! The reality is that you cannot do what you cannot do.

Sometimes we feel overwhelmed or unable to fix everything that is wrong in our lives or in our world. It is then that we must do what we can. We can't do more than this, but nor should we do less.

What can I do today?

What I can do
is usually far more than
I think I can do.

145 - Don't do list

As well as having a list of goals to achieve, it can also be useful to have a list of things to avoid or not do. Things like distractions and time-wasters or bad habits that tend to stop you achieving your positive goals. These may be events, places or situations that have been problematic before, or relationships that bring out the worst in you. It may include food or drinks that are bad for you or anything that is the opposite of what you are trying to achieve. 'Know thy enemy' can be a useful strategy. Don't buy those biscuits. Don't turn on the TV. Walk away from that person, place or event. Stay away from that shop or website. Know what you really don't want to do and don't do it!

What would I have on my Don't Do list?

Knowing what to do
and what not to do
are two sides
of the same animal.

146 - Pray!

Don't underestimate the power of prayer and positive thinking.

Recruit family and friends to support and encourage you.

Get regular hugs, pokes, texts or whatever reminds you that you are loved and being thought of.

Doing it by yourself is not an option. Use your support crew, whoever they may be, when you need them. Do the same for your friends when they need you. You are in this together and together you can make it!

Who can I recruit to be part of my support team?

Pray as though everything depended on God.
Work as though everything depended on you.
Augustine

147 - Remember

Make an effort to remember these times as you come to the end of your school days. Many new experiences await you and over time memories of school will fade. Keep a few mementos, photos and tokens to help you remember. This is a part of your life. Write down your feelings. Keep the contact details of friends. Don't dismiss all of the things that have been a part of making you who you are now. Hold on to some of your foundations.

What do I want to keep and remember?

*We will leave
and grow and change,
but the past
will always be a part
of who we become.*

148 - Begin it now!

It is never too late to start. If you haven't been doing enough work, study or exercise up until now, make a start. Begin today! Good habits take time to establish, but every step in the right direction is a step in the right direction. A big effort at the end is better than no effort at all. Starting now is better than not starting. You never know, you might surprise yourself. Don't give up on yourself. Each new day brings new beginnings.

What do I need to start doing today?

*Now is always
the best time
to start doing
anything worth doing.*

149 - Commencement!

American students don't have a graduation ceremony. Instead, they call it a 'Commencement' ceremony. This is the beginning of the rest of your life. Don't waste time looking back at what was or regretting something that did or didn't happen in the past. Look forward with hope and anticipation. This is the start of something new and big and exciting (and perhaps a little bit frightening too). Stride out into your future knowing that you have the encouragement, love and support of your teachers, parents, family, peers and friends.

What are you looking forward to commencing?

*Tomorrow and tomorrow and tomorrow –
your life goes on,
so much to look forward to,
so many memories to create.*

150 - Keep learning!

Graduating from school does not mean graduating from life – there is much to learn and there always will be. Take pleasure in continuing to develop knowledge and skills in areas that interest you. Be curious. Keep in touch with new developments and ideas in whatever field you find yourself in. Stretch your comfort zone and don't limit yourself to what you have to know to do your job. Life is full of new lessons. Live and learn!

What is the next action?

As long as you are alive
there is always more to learn.
This is a good thing.

150+ My Own Life Lessons, Questions & Quotes

My life lesson: _____

_____

_____

_____

_____

_____

_____

_____

My life lesson: _____

_____

_____

_____

_____

_____

_____

_____

My life lesson: _____

_____

_____

_____

_____

_____

_____

_____

_____

My life lesson: _____

_____

_____

_____

_____

_____

_____

_____

_____

My life lesson: _____

_____

_____

_____

_____

_____

_____

_____

My life lesson: _____

_____

_____

_____

_____

_____

_____

_____

My life lesson: _____

_____

_____

_____

_____

_____

_____

_____

_____

_____

My life lesson: _____

_____

_____

_____

_____

_____

_____

_____

_____

_____

My life lesson: _____

_____

_____

_____

_____

_____

_____

_____

_____

My life lesson: _____

_____

_____

_____

_____

_____

_____

_____

_____

www.ingramcontent.com/pod-product-compliance
Lightning Source LLC
Chambersburg PA
CBHW062110290426
44110CB00023B/2769